THE STORY
OF
RADIO FORTH

Fiona McAuslane

KU-064-837

Paul Harris Publishing
in association with
Radio Forth

First published January 1985
to celebrate the Tenth Anniversary of Radio Forth
by Paul Harris Publishing
40 York Place
Edinburgh
in association with Radio Forth

© Copyright Radio Forth 1985

ISBN 0 86228 105 9

Printed in Scotland by John G Eccles Printers Ltd

THE STORY OF RADIO FORTH

Radio Forth staff outside the station's premises in Forth Street.

CONTENTS

Richard Findlay, managing director of Radio Forth.

PREFACE

Writing this preface to 'The Story of Radio Forth' is easier than I had at first imagined and it is certainly a pleasure and privilege I never envisaged ten surprisingly short years ago.

Because this book is the story of Radio Forth, it seemed to me that I should use this opportunity to express thanks and gratitude to all those who have played a part, both large and small, in one of the most successful, exciting and always stimulating broadcasting companies in the U.K. Many names appear on the following pages but there are, of course, so many more and none more important than the hundreds of thousands of loyal listeners who form the essential 'bedrock' of the Radio Forth family.

No story of Radio Forth could be complete without the men and women who make up the Board of Directors of the company and who, under the skilful Chairmanship of Max Harper Gow, have guided the company over the years. Max became our Chairman a few months after I took over as Managing Director and the company and I owe much to him.

Other directors who made an enormous contribution to the company in the early days included Brian Lascelles of John Menzies Holdings, David Snedden and Roger Ridley-Thomas of Scotsman Publications, Peter Balfour and, of course, the late and sorely missed Sandy Brown. Sir James Mackay, our first Chairman, and Christopher Lucas, our first Managing Director, continue to take a fond interest in the company to which they contributed so much.

Thank you then to all who have served and continue to serve Radio Forth — directors, staff, freelance contributors. Thanks also to our shareholders and advertisers who make the whole thing possible, but thank *you* particularly for your support and loyalty, which we hope we can continue to justify for the next decade.

Richard Findlay

INTRODUCTION

It is 8 o'clock on a cold, dark, winter morning. The people of Forth Country are still slumbering but, in a brightly lit building in Edinburgh's New Town, there is tense excitement and everyone is extremely wide awake.

For the date is January 22nd, 1975 and the airwaves are about to be filled with a new sound — the sound of Radio Forth.

As the sleepy world outside gradually comes to life, the atmosphere in the studios in Forth Street reaches fever pitch. People will be wakening and turning to their radios to establish that the outside world is still there. Radio Forth will undergo its first test at 6.00 a.m. precisely!

One year had been spent in preparing for this moment, when, at last, the silence was broken by the words: "This, for the very first time, is Radio Forth." The words were followed by the Radio Forth song and the first record, "January" — a chart-topping number by a local group called Pilot.

The staff and directors watched and listened anxiously as their baby, Radio Forth, took its first steps towards the arms and ears of the listeners they wanted so desperately to please. There had been plenty of advance publicity for the new station but now the moment of truth had arrived; would the listeners tune in to the new service? Test transmissions of Tchaikovsky's 1812 Overture had been broadcast in the weeks previously to help people to find their new station on 96.8 VHF and 194m medium wave.

That was TEN years ago. Now Radio Forth is an established part of life in East Central Scotland and who could imagine the airwaves without that familiar "Close to You" jingle, the cheerful chat of the friendly presenters, the local news broadcasts and discussion programmes on wider issues linked with news from around the world? Radio Forth has built up a loyal band of listeners, has had its good times and not so good times but always pursued its aim to inform and entertain.

The infant station's early steps were financially shaky but within three years it had established a sound financial base and gone from strength to strength. It has made a reputation as an innovative radio station, constantly breaking new ground and trying out new ideas. It has also proved how useful a local radio station can be to the community it serves and has become a familiar friend to its listeners.

RADIO ROOTS

The roots of much of today's commercial radio lie in America where, in 1946, a radio man decided to meet the competition from television with what he called Top 40 Format Radio. His presenters played the most popular records of the moment and found they were providing a service which people wanted. Gradually, this type of radio spread throughout the USA and Canada. Inevitably, the idea travelled across the Atlantic and was established in the UK via the pirate radio stations.

The success of those stations — remember the original Radio Scotland, Radio Caroline, Radio London? — proved that there was a place for this kind of broadcasting in this country. Some poured scorn on the idea of commercial radio and lined up solidly behind the BBC with its reputation for 'quality' programmes. But a great many others welcomed the breath of fresh air blowing around prim Auntie BBC's ankles and backed the idea of local radio to provide much needed competition.

The election of a Tory government in 1970 gave the amber light to commercial radio. A White Paper, entitled *An Alternative Service of Local Broadcasting*, was published and envisaged a total of 60 stations. It pointed out that local broadcasting had a lot to commend it while local advertising would provide a valuable service to consumers. The Independent Television Authority began making plans for the introduction of Independent Local Radio (ILR) and, in 1972, a new Act extended the ITA's functions to cover local sound broadcasting. The ITA became the IBA — the Independent Broadcasting Authority.

The IBA controls the output of commercial television and radio, ensuring that a high standard is maintained and a good balance between information and music achieved. They rent the transmitters to the radio stations and charge a secondary rental when a company's profits exceed 5 per cent of advertising revenue, thus ensuring that commercial radio can never be regarded as a 'goldmine'.

The BBC, naturally, was watching those developments with interest. It had already reacted to competition from the pirates by re-organising its radio services into Radios 1, 2, 3 and 4, which replaced the familiar Home, Light and Third programmes. So, it provided a pop channel and, shortly afterwards, established eight local radio stations and more followed. But the advance of local commercial radio could not be halted now and in June 1972 the locations of 26 ILR stations were announced.

The largest centres of population — London, Glasgow, Birmingham and Manchester — were to have the first stations. In late 1973 the two London stations opened: LBC, an all news and information station, then Capital, an entertainment station. Radio Clyde opened soon after, as did Piccadilly in Manchester. Four more stations were created in 1974 and Radio Forth followed in 1975.

The public demand for independent radio had been headed by the politicians, broadcasters were now ready and willing to try out their talents on a new medium and forward thinking and entrepreneurial companies and individuals were found to invest in the new enterprise.

TO WIN A FRANCHISE

In Edinburgh, four groups were preparing plans to persuade the IBA that they were the most suitable people to run a radio station in the East Central Scotland region.

David Snedden, Managing Director of The Scotsman Publications Ltd., had persuaded several influential names to join a consortium — Scottish and Newcastle Breweries, John Menzies, Christian Salvesen and merchant bankers, Edward Bates and Co. Ltd. The first meeting was held in March, 1973 at the offices of Scottish and Newcastle in Holyrood and, as David Snedden explains: "The companies agreed to put £10,000 each into the venture and, if we didn't win the franchise, the money would be written off. We thought we looked too much like high-power big business so we asked the Co-op to join us to provide the link between business and the people. We then had to think of local individuals with special talents who would be useful on the board."

The consortium would have welcomed Professor Michael Swann, then Principal of Edinburgh University, onto their board and a letter was written asking him if he was willing to serve. He stalled a little and finally wrote apologising for having to turn down the offer in favour of another — a request from Prime Minister Edward Heath that he take over as Chairman of the BBC!

It was agreed that the Board should be representative of entertainment, sport, education, politics, the interests of women and the public at large. So, when the board was formed it included George Foulkes, now a Labour MP, but then Chairman of Lothian Region's Education Committee; Donald Ford, an ex-footballer and successful accountant; Wendy Blakey, to represent the area around Falkirk where she was involved with many aspects of life; Bob MacPherson, representing Scottish Television; actress Lennox Milne; jazz musician and acoustician, Sandy Brown, who was also an architect and was to prove invaluable in finding and creating the right location for the radio station.

The first priority at this time was to prepare an application for the franchise which would persuade the IBA that the Radio Forth consortium's plans were the best. IBA guidelines stressed the importance of involving local people with local expertise. They also expected to see a significant output of news and information and programmes of a generally high standard, providing a proper balance.

There were strict rules about the amount of advertising allowed — a maximum of nine minutes of commercials in one hour of broadcasting.

The consortium's plan envisaged programme segments throughout the day with music interspersed with feature material. This would be the format from 6.00 a.m. until 6.00 p.m. and the music would cater for middle-of-the-road tastes.

In the evening the programming would be more specialised with segments for teenagers, perhaps an open-line on community problems and some light classical music.

The board studied previous applications in other areas and came to the conclusion that the IBA would be looking for a firm Scottish base to the application with the emphasis on local involvement. Long and

Wendy Blakey

heated discussions were held on the subject of a name for the radio station. Radio Edinburgh had been rejected at the beginning as it excluded Fife, Central Region and the Lothians which were all part of the transmission area.

Wendy Blakey explained: "The one common link which the whole region had was the Forth and, finally, we all agreed that it was the logical choice."

So, Radio Forth and Forth Country entered the language.

There were problems with the name as it was similar to Forth Radio Network which was the local hospital broadcasting service. However, they had never registered the name and were willing to accept Radio Forth's offer of payment of the costs involved in changing their name.

As local radio was so new to Britain there were few professionals in the field to call on for advice. The BBC local radio stations could not be used as a model for they opted in and out of national programming — local commercial radio would have to stand firmly on its own feet. Across the Atlantic the Americans and Canadians were old hands in the business with thousands of commercial radio stations which had been broadcasting for decades. It was the obvious place to look for advice.

A Canadian company — Selkirk Communications Ltd. — offered their services as consultants. They had wide experience in broadcasting and had been involved with LBC in London. Kenneth Baker, their vice-president in charge of operations in the UK, was the man who passed on the benefit of his experience to the Radio Forth consortium. He organised training sessions for the vital meeting with the IBA when the Radio Forth representatives would have to face a grilling and make a strong case for their suitability to run a local commercial radio station.

Roger Ridley-Thomas of *The Scotsman* and Brian Lascelles of John Menzies, travelled to Canada and spent two weeks watching local radio in action. In early September 1973 a meeting was held in the North British Hotel, Edinburgh and Sir James McKay, a former Lord Provost of Edinburgh, accepted the post of Chairman of Radio Forth.

The strongest competition seemed to come from the Waverley Broadcasting Company, which had been brought together by Richard Findlay — later to figure strongly in the Radio Forth story. Waverley was backed by British Caledonian, Morgan Grampian, the Scottish Farmers' Union, British Lion Films, Nairns of Kirkcaldy, educational publishers Holmes McDougall, and the Scottish Braille Press. Nicholas Fairbairn and actress Moira Shearer were two well-known personalities involved with the Waverley consortium, along with Richard Findlay.

The two other groups were eliminated at the first hearing of the IBA to consider the application, leaving Radio Forth and Waverley to battle it out.

The hearing was held at the end of November, 1973 and seven board members attended — Sir James McKay, Peter Balfour, David Snedden, George Foulkes, Wendy Blakey, Douglas MacDonald and Bob MacPherson. Practice sessions with Ken Baker continued until the final hearing and the team arrived feeling nervous but confident. Awaiting their appointed time for the interrogation in London's Hyde Park Hotel, they found themselves sitting a few yards away from their rivals, the Waverley team. They kept the conversation low in case any vital piece of information was picked up by the opposition.

Wendy Blakey remembers: "Nicky Fairbairn was dressed in flamboyant 18th century gear and Moira Shearer looked very glamorous. We could only hope that the content of our application would outshine their appearance."

David Snedden recalls that the hearing got off to a sticky start: "Lord Aylestone was in the chair and he asked a question which no-one understood. Fortunately, a lady member of the interviewing team intervened and smoothed out the situation."

As the franchise team made their way home to Edinburgh there was a snowstorm and, as she looked out of the aircraft window, Wendy began to doubt if she was going to see her family again: "Conditions were awful and, when I saw Lennox Milne take out her rosary, I became convinced that we wouldn't make it and could only think what a rotten Christmas the children would have." However, they all arrived home safely to celebrate Christmas and await the news from the IBA.

In fact, the news came on Christmas Eve — they had won the franchise!

David Snedden 'phoned everyone with the news and a first meeting of the board was organised for March 5th, 1974.

ONE YEAR TO D-DAY

There was no time for a champagne reception in these early days for a great deal had to be accomplished in the next twelve months. It was going to cost £450,000 to set up the radio station. Staff had to be recruited, premises found and equipped.

The search for a Chief Executive began and 37 applications were recieved. The successful applicant was Christopher Lucas, an accountant working for the IBA. Christopher began work in May and was installed in a basement office of The Scotsman Publications with an A4 pad and a pencil. He was joined shortly after by another accountant, Alan Wilson; an engineer, Jim Donaldson; a programme controller, Richard Findlay (recruited from the Waverley consortium); and head of news, Tom Steele.

Richard's interest in radio had begun in his student days at the Royal Scottish Academy of Music and Drama. He subsequently worked for the BBC and the pirate station, Radio London. He then worked in Saudi Arabia with the broadcasting services there, while helping in the launch of a weekly English language tabloid newspaper for the country.

"I was watching developments in radio in Britain with interest and I was waiting for the opportunity to get into commercial radio — especially in my home town of Edinburgh," he explains.

"In fact, I came home a little too soon and filled in the

time working for the Central Office of Information's overseas radio service and then with Capital — one of the first ILR stations. I got the Waverley consortium together and was bitterly disappointed when we failed to get the franchise for Edinburgh but was delighted when the call came to join Radio Forth."

Alan Wilson had joined as financial controller one month before Richard and he describes how he spent his first day working in the bar of the St James Hotel because he had no office space.

"In the evening there was a meeting at Scottish and Newcastle Breweries and the financial projections were being discussed," he remembers.

"The atmosphere was pessimistic and someone said we might as well give up now! And I had just left a steady job with Collins the publishers."

However, Alan had worked with Granada Television and found the atmosphere in broadcasting stimulating and fun and was prepared to take his chances with Radio Forth.

Jim Donaldson was an experienced engineer and did an excellent job in planning the studios and equipment for the station. Having seen the station through its first months he gave up city life to set up his own business on the island of Arran.

Tom Steele was a journalist who had begun his career in newspapers, at one point having the distinction of being the youngest lobby correspondent at Westminster. He moved to BBC Scotland in the late Sixties and worked in television before moving to one of the new BBC local radio stations — Radio Sheffield.

Tom found the medium he loved best when he discovered radio and the prospect of commercial radio was an exciting one. He joined Radio Clyde in its planning stages and was familiar with all the problems involved in setting up a radio newsroom when he joined Forth in 1974.

20

The "studios" of Radio Forth before the station's opening
in 1975.

Radio Clyde had proved an instant success but the
Radio Forth board realised that they had a different
audience to deal with. Their area was more frag-
mented and would take longer to pull together. The
people of Fife might take some time to identify with a
station covering the Lothians and people in Central
Region might feel they had little in common with
Edinburgh. As predicted, it did take longer for Forth to
build up its audience but, when they did, it proved a
loyal audience and the gradual build-up was to have
the advantage of creating a secure base.

Meanwhile, the search for suitable premises had

ended with a decision to move into Forth House, Forth Street on the fringe of the New Town. (This was to create problems when the station wanted to advertise its presence on the outside of the building as a discreet brass name-plate is the only type of advertising approved of in Edinburgh's prestigious New Town). The board had decided that the studios and offices must be somewhere near the centre of town and it seemed like fate when the Forth address came on to the market.

Sandy Brown used his skills as an architect and expert in acoustics to examine the building and report on its suitability, plus the cost of conversion. The figure came to £120,000 and the rental of the building was to be between £20,000 and £25,000.

At the beginning, the radio station occupied the basement and three upper floors but it soon became clear that all this space was unnecessary and parts of the building were gradually leased out to other companies. Forth now occupies just the ground floor and basement plus a suite of offices at the rear of the building.

As engineers and workmen toiled in the basements, laying over eight miles of cable and creating three studios, two control rooms and a master control room, the programme planning went ahead on the echoing top floor with its staff of five. Already there was a steady stream of applications to join Radio Forth and gradually a team of presenters, reporters, engineers, sales and office staff were recruited.

Freda Todd was appointed sales manager — an appointment which met Christopher's aim to have at least one woman on his management team.

On December 2nd, 1974, when the new staff began to arrive, Richard recalls: "Everything looked great on paper. We had everything worked out and could foresee no problems — until the staff arrived. Then chaos reigned."

Tom Steele remembers the growing excitement: "I had come straight from helping to build the station of Radio Clyde and I knew the scale of the job ahead of us but we were all brimming with enthusiasm and prepared to put all our efforts into this new venture."

Tom couldn't resist a trip round the large office on a dinky new motor scooter which had arrived for the news team.

Steve Hamilton was one of the first disc jockeys to report for duty and he was determined not to reveal just how green he was on the subject of radio. He recalls: "Jay Crawford arrived soon after me and began asking a lot of questions about equipment etc. I nudged him in the ribs and said 'Don't let them know we are quite so clueless'."

With few experienced radio men around, there was no choice but to recruit enthusiastic amateurs. However, all the staff were professionals in their own fields of entertainment, music, sales, news and engineering, even if they were new to broadcasting. The presenters were anxious to spend as much time as possible in the nearly completed studios, familiarising themselves with the equipment and rehearsing.

"There were three weeks of dry runs for the presenters and competition for studio time was hot," says Steve Hamilton. "I used to come in at 4.00 a.m. to get extra time in the studio."

Steve, like Jay, and one or two of the other presenters, was an ex-student of drama college. Jay Crawford's name had been considered for the prestigious role of Jesus Christ in the film *Jesus of Nazareth* and, when that big opportunity fell through, he sent a demo-tape off to Radio Forth: "When I got the job I thought I would last six months — and I'm still here ten years later," he says.

"At the beginning I saw myself as another John Peel,

23

CHRISTOPHER JOHN   JAY CRAWFORD   BARBARA BROWN   DAVE ANTHONY
    MIKE GOWER   STEVE HAMILTON   DOUGIE KING   IAN ANDERSON

A picture of the presenters who were with Forth for its launch in 1975.

playing heavy rock music — rather avant-garde. I was delighted to be given an evening show called Edinburgh Rock. I was not so pleased to hear that Richard's idea for the show was to appeal to the teeny boppers and I was to play Bay City Rollers type of material — Sweet Edinburgh Rock! So much for my 'cool' image.

"My DJ technique was gleaned from advice I heard from Tony Blackburn — 'Keep it short'. I knew very little when I started. The engineers explained how the equipment worked and Dave Anthony — one of the DJs with some experience — gave us tips on presentation."

Richard Findlay's programme schedule had been ready since October 1974 and the bill was to be £135,650. Test transmissions were going out and the on-air date of January 22nd, 1975 was fixed.

It was important to make people aware of the new radio station and special promotions and advertising campaigns were organised. At the time Richard, addressing his potential listeners, summed up his plans this way: "As a station we are making an enormous effort to give you the kind of programmes you will enjoy listening to. For example, we've got our rollicking drama serial — Deacon Brodie — every weekday morning.

"There is Swop Shop, where you can 'phone in and exchange your second-hand goods with each other. We have competitions with attractive prizes. We have comedy, quiz and magazine programmes. There is something for the children with Roundabout on Sunday morning, and something for the elderly with Those Were the Days on Sunday evenings.

"News comes in on the hour with headlines on the half hour during peak periods and our extended news wraps at 1.00 p.m. and 5 p.m. to keep you abreast of local developments. We even have our own Poet Laureate to 'McGonogallise' you all in verse every week.

"We have set ourselves a gigantic task but, with your help, we can build the bridge so sorely needed in this part of Scotland. We will certainly do our best, the rest is up to you; we're waiting, so come and join us.

"TOGETHER WE'LL BLOW AWAY THE COBWEBS THAT HAVE BEEN ALLOWED TO GATHER AROUND SCOTTISH RADIO TRANSMITTERS."

Tom Steele explained the station's plans for the news and current affairs service in this way: "Listeners will hear, for the first time, a 'rolling news'. It's a new technique to get news to the microphone much quicker than before. It also enables the listener to hear the radio reporter at work, particularly on a big story running throughout the day.

"Local radio has the advantage over all other news media — it can bring you the news as it happens. We intend to take full advantage of this ability to be first with the news.

"Not only will Radio Forth be rolling local news but Scottish, national and international news as well. We have the ability to go anywhere in the world through special broadcast lines — some of them via satellites — to capture the sound of major world events."

Hamish Wilson, who had been in the theatre and broadcasting with Richard, was the arts producer and he promised there would be nothing elitist about his part in programming: "The Radio Forth arts chat won't be a bit toffee-nosed or cliquish or obscure. I'm much more concerned with letting people know what's happening around them and suggesting they don't know it till they've tried it, whether it's the latest London movie or an exhibition of young people's paintings. We want to let people hear what's on at their local theatre, what new books are coming out, who's weaving what and what's new in pottery."

The Deacon Brodie series was planned for serialisation each morning while Bram Stoker's *Dracula* and other novels were to be broadcast in instalments late at night.

Nancy Mitchell would host a daily magazine programme going out between 3 and 3.30, there was to be a police spot to highlight information about crime in the area and on Wednesday evenings the Forth Line offered listeners in Forth Country a new experience — they could broadcast themselves by dialling what is now a familiar number — 031 557 0194.

A View From Earth was established at this time as a religious magazine programme and is generally rec-

News room staff and presenters pose for a picture during the hectic weeks of preparation to go on air.

ognised now as one of the best there is on radio — it has a host of awards to prove the point. Not that our religious affairs contributors like to boast, you understand!

The board held their first AGM on December 31st and their first meeting in Forth House was held on Friday, January 10th. Christopher Lucas was able to report the programme department's successful dry-runs and that several programmes were already recorded for future transmission.

No big party was scheduled for January 22nd, the launching day, but the adrenalin was flowing strongly as it approached. The months leading up to the station's opening had been exciting and fun for the young staff and everyone was prepared to put all their efforts into the final preparations. Camp beds were installed in the offices as the big day approached and staff snatched just a few hours sleep before getting back to work.

Few of the staff slept on January 21st and it was a relief to everyone when the magic moment finally arrived — and passed without a hitch. Radio Forth had arrived. Would it be a success or a failure? Only time would tell. The sleepless, hectic pace took its toll. Richard lost his voice for a time but the relentless pace continued and regular slugs of medication restored his vocal chords sufficiently to make the opening announcement at 6.00 a.m. on January 22nd, 1975.

FIRST YEARS

The station broadcast from 6.00 a.m. until midnight each day and the broadcasting hours were extended to 1.00 a.m. in March, 1975. Now Radio Forth broadcasts from 5.00 a.m. until 2.00 a.m. each day.

The familiar format, which continues to prove successful today, consisted of blocks of programmes from 6.00 a.m. until 6.00 p.m. — the Breakfast Show, the Mid-Morning Show, the Lunchtime Show and the Afternoon Show and so on. More specialised programmes were broadcast in the evenings.

The station lost a valued friend in jazz clarinetist, Sandy Brown, who died tragically at the early age of 46 in March, 1975.

George Foulkes had been appointed Deputy Chairman of the Radio Forth Board but he soon realised that IBA rules were interfering with his political role. Being a member of the board placed restrictions on his freedom to broadcast and, as Chairman of the Education Committee, he had to be available to comment. He resigned for this reason.

The first audience research was done in May 1975 and indicated that Forth had a healthy 40% share of the audience in the area. Meanwhile, there were the inevitable staff changes as things began to settle down and some people found that they couldn't measure up to the demands of radio.

Sandy Webster

Ex-newspaper editor, Sandy Webster, accepted the exacting job of hosting the Sunday morning 'phone-in show. His brother, Jack, is famous in Canada for his 'phone-in shows and his frank — if not downright rude — manner of dealing with callers. When he visited brother Sandy's show at Forth he was warned that Forth listeners were unlikely to appreciate his abrasive style and he toned it down slightly. Sandy remained at Radio Forth for several years before handing over to Clarke Tait who, in turn, handed over to Margo MacDonald who handles her difficult task skilfully.

Margo MacDonald

DIFFICULT DAYS

Meanwhile, there were clouds on the horizon. The financial picture was not rosy in early 1976 and the board was worried. A meeting of executives was held in the Royal Scot Hotel so that Christopher could explain the position and announce budget cuts of 50 per cent. As they were half-way through the year at this time, it meant dramatic cuts. Shareholders Selkirk Communications had promised more cash help but only if their own man could come in and examine what was happening. Canadian, Robbie Dunn, spent some time at the station but found little to criticise apart from a few administrative details.

Richard Findlay recalls that, at the beginning, it was estimated that the company would take three years to find its financial feet and "that is precisely what we did, almost to the day. I don't think it was ever anticipated that we would make money immediately but we have made a trading profit every year since 1977."

Christopher Lucas had been a popular boss and was liked by all the staff but he discovered that running a commercial radio station was not for him and, in March 1977, he resigned and now heads the Royal Society of Arts in London.

Richard Findlay became Managing Director and everything in the station was shaken up. A new programme schedule was prepared and the presenters instructed to tighten up their style.

Richard Findlay, surrounded by the staff of Radio Forth, presents Christopher Lucas with his farewell gift in 1977.

David Snedden remembers those difficult times: "The station was simply spending too much and was over-staffed so changes had to be made. We also felt that the presenters were tending to let their egos get between them and the audience."

Derek Gorman was appointed Sales Manager. He is an Ulster man and had worked as sales manager of *The Scotsman* before returning to Northern Ireland for a spell prior to taking up the Radio Forth post. Ninety-nine per cent of the revenue of a commercial station is brought in by advertising and Derek's role was a key one. He prepared a report for the board on the situation as he saw it.

On the plus side he mentioned the good listening sound and audience of the station. On the minus side he discovered a distrust of local radio as an advertising

Derek Gorman, sales director of Radio Forth for some years.

medium and he found that many of the sales team were inadequately trained and not providing a good service to the advertisers. Just as Richard was having ruthlessly to apply himself to cutting costs on the programming side, Derek had to improve the sales department's performance to attract more advertisers to Forth.

By January 1977 the staff had been cut from 68 to 46 and costs had been trimmed all round. A tighter ship was now launched on the airwaves and the rough patch was over.

The loss which the company made in 1975-76 was the last it ever made.

Richard gives the staff a great deal of credit: "When they realised the situation, the entire staff was behind us in helping to make cuts and, by penny-pinching on all sides — cutting down on 'phone calls, stationery and all unnecessary expenses — we managed to meet the target."

A forecast loss of over £50,000 for 1976-77 was turned round to a profit of £20,000 in just six months.

SNOWLINE AND OPEN LINE

The winter of 1978-79 was a highlight in the Radio Forth story.

A combination of blizzard conditions plus a strike by road gritting supervisors in the Lothian Region created a crisis. Over the New Year holiday weekend 'phone calls came pouring into the radio station from people in trouble: people with burst water pipes who could not contact plumbers; old people trapped in their homes and running out of provisions; hospital staff who could not get to work and were asking for transport. The terrible road conditions meant that public transport was in chaos.

The newsroom staff 'phoned Tom Steele at home to let him know that they were deluged with calls for help and he realised that the station would have to do something about the situation.

"I drove into the office and, as I travelled along the treacherous roads, I realised how serious the situation was. Vehicles could not move because the roads were like ice-rinks. There was no gritting being done in Edinburgh, East and West Lothian. I 'phoned Richard and we agreed to scrap our normal programming and, so, the now famous *Snowline* was launched."

Tom broadcast an appeal for staff to come into the office and the response was immediate. The whole situation was exacerbated by the fact that it was a holiday weekend and social services were underman-

Tom Steele, programme director.

ned. When people could not raise official help, they called Radio Forth.

"Hundreds of volunteers came into the station offering their help," added Tom. "There were plumbers to deal with the dozens of burst pipes; there were people who had chain tyres and could therefore get about on the ungritted roads; there were offers of food and blankets for people who could not get out and about."

There had been plenty of talk in the past of local radio's value to the community — here was an opportunity to prove its worth. The station was on air constantly for 96 hours dealing with the calls and liaising between the helpers and those who needed help. It also proved to be compulsive listening and won for the station a new respect in the community.

A newspaper said afterwards: "It was heady stuff. For four days the station was the centre of the universe for those who sat beleagured, stranded and slightly pickled, watching the white world outside go by." It went on: "It was radio journalism without the inevitable scripted clichés; a kind of inspired media mayhem." The writer ended: "I never thought I would see the day when I would get a plumber through a radio station. Radio Forth, on behalf of myself and my frozen pipes, I am extremely grateful."

Snowline proved that good neighbours still existed. A young girl 'phoned to say that the shelter for her 32 year-old horse had collapsed under the weight of the snow — a team of joiners offered to rebuild the shelter to save the elderly animal.

A farmer asked for skis and sledges to take fodder to his sheep, the Royal Hospital for Sick Children requested milk supplies as they were running short and were soon 'snowed under' with pintas.

In Kendal a farmer picked up Radio Forth and asked the station to broadcast an appeal to his shepherds to return home from the hills where they were trying to

The Snowline theme was used for the Radio Forth float in the 1979 Festival Cavalcade.

save their flocks from the terrible weather conditions. Miraculously — probably due to the freak weather conditions — they picked up the messages on their walkie talkies and all returned safely before they were overtaken by blizzards.

Local cafes kept the volunteers and staff at Forth Street supplied with rolls, coffee and hot potatoes.

"It became clear that 99 per cent of the population in our area were tuning into *Snowline*," says Richard. "It really established local radio as an essential part of the community with an important role to play in emergency conditions. People were cut off in their homes with only their radios and telephones as a means of communication. The emergency was confined to this area where the gritters were not operating so the national broadcasting organisations were more or less ignoring the situation."

The *Snowline* brought a response from the public which warmed the hearts of everyone in Forth Country. East coasters had dispelled the myth that they are cold, unhelpful people. Without a warm and caring community there would have been no *Snowline*.

Even *The Scotsman* newspaper — always reluctant to acknowledge the young, lively radio station in its area — had to grudgingly admit: "There can be no snide minimising of the job that Radio Forth did for the community it serves in the East of Scotland during the area's snow-bound New Year."

The *Snowline* also brought awards to the radio station. The Lord Provost, Lothian Region and Kirkcaldy District laid on receptions to express their thanks and the listeners in their thousands sent in messages of appreciation to the Forth staff and the volunteers.

The whole exercise led the Radio Forth team to another new concept in radio — the Open Line.

The *Snowline* had made them aware of the number of lonely people, isolated in their homes, who looked on the radio as their only friend. The idea of a problem column of the air was born.

There had been advice programmes broadcast before but they were generally on practical subjects with experts offering practical tips.

Forth's revolutionary idea was to invite people to 'phone in with their personal problems and discuss them with sympathetic and friendly counsellors.

Reaction to the idea was mixed. The people professionally involved with dealing with problems — the police, social workers and local counsellors, plus the medical profession — were invited to meetings to discuss the idea.

Social workers were suspicious of a service which might interfere with their field of activity; churchmen expressed doubts and thought it might encourage voyeurism; professional broadcasters thought it was madness to replace a popular late-night music show with three hours discussing human problems . . . the idea was to broadcast the *Open Line* from 11.00 p.m. until 2.00 a.m. on a Saturday night.

However, Richard and Tom stuck by their idea and were given backing by the board.

Social workers who approved of the programme pointed out that Saturday night was the worst night of the week for those with problems. It was the traditional evening for socialising and, if you were alone, you felt your isolation more keenly. Also, it was the night when people usually went drinking and that in itself raised problems.

It was decided to run the *Open Line* during the winter months, starting in October 1979.

The counsellors prefer to remain anonymous and callers give only their christian names on air.

Andy has been a counsellor since the programme started and he describes the aim of the Open Line:

"We provide a friend for lonely and troubled people

41

at a time in the weekend when people feel particularly alone with their problems.

"In no sense does the programme set out to provide a social work agency or professional counselling but rather the radio equivalent of the good friend you never realised lived next door."

To accusations of pandering to an unhealthy interest in other people's problems, Andy responds by pointing out:

"It depends how the programme is handled, the level of advice offered and whether there is a genuine attempt at caring."

All counsellors involved in the programme are highly qualified.

The range of problems they have to deal with in an evening can be illustrated by one typical programme when callers included a woman whose whole family was affected by multiple sclerosis, a young lad hooked on drugs, a battered wife, a man who had found his wife in bed with another man that evening, a school girl frightened by the attention of a male, married teacher and a homosexual trying to find a way of telling his parents of his problem.

It is a sad catalogue of human misery but they are problems which cannot be ignored and there is ample evidence from follow-up correspondence to show that many callers are given real help by the *Open Line* counsellors.

A radio critic wrote that she admired Radio Forth for "their nerve in taking the risks and their skill in handling them."

On one or two occasions other help has been contacted by the *Open Line* team when it seemed that someone was on the verge of suicide or a situation was reaching a dangerous crisis.

The two counsellors are backed up by an engineer and two others who answer 'phones, weeding out imposters and helping callers to clarify what they most want to talk about.

Richard sees it this way: "Listening to the radio is something anyone can do — there is no great technical feat involved in switching on. Finding the agency which can help you with a problem is not so easy. Even if you locate the correct agency you then have to pluck up the courage to approach the people there who will be strangers. Our counsellors are familiar voices on the radio each week and become like friends whom people can confide in. We see ourselves as the initial step people take in solving their problems."

The programme does not try to take the place of the helping agencies — it simply provides a stepping stone to assist people to find the right kind of help with their problems. It is another method of building bridges between people in the community.

There are still those who accuse the programme of exploiting the problems of individuals for public entertainment and the people involved in the programme are well aware of the dangers but feel that, on balance, the series does far more good than harm.

Listening figures for the *Open Line* have soared and the response from the public has been appreciative. Awards have been heaped on the programme and perhaps the greatest compliment is that the idea has been adopted by other radio stations.

Andy admits: "Counselling on this programme is radically different from normal counselling. You have to have the ability to broadcast successfully and establish a one-to-one communication which is free from the barriers of remoteness, irritation and oratory. We describe it as 'breakthrough' counselling. Talking about a problem reduces the terror it creates and, having been accepted by another person, the callers feel confident enough to go on to other recommended agencies."

One example of someone freed from twelve years of misery by her call to the Open Line was a professional woman tormented by a social worker's confidential report which she had read after her son was convicted of murder. In the report — which she knew she should not have read — she was blamed for the way her son was. When she brought her feelings of guilt out into the open and sought further help it was subsequently proved that she was, in fact, an exemplary and long-suffering mother. She wrote a few weeks after her call to express her thanks for the help and peace she had found after bottling the problem up for those twelve years.

SEEN AND HEARD

A radio station has to make its listeners aware that it is THERE to be heard. You can't see the station as you can a newspaper or a television set. Newspapers are notoriously mean about the amount of space they will devote to the daily programme schedule so the radio stations have to mount their own promotions to remind listeners of their existence. These promotions often lead to hilarious incidents and provide staff and listeners with a load of laughs.

One of Forth's first promotions was an unmitigated disaster and left the station with egg — or haggis — on its face. Burns Night was just three nights after the station's opening on January 22nd and it seemed a good idea to have a promotion linked with Burns. A haggis, 20 feet long by 10 feet wide, was ordered from the famous haggis makers, McSween's of Bruntsfield. It was filled with the traditional liver, lights and oatmeal and loaded on to a lorry.

The plan was for the gaily decorated haggis to tour Forth Country so that listeners could guess its weight — the winner would, of course, receive a prize. Over 700 bright balloons were tied to the haggis along with ribbons and banners, making a scene to brighten a dreich January day. The first stop was to be in Fife and, on the final day, the lorry would arrive in time for a Burns supper in Dalkeith.

Things began to go wrong as soon as the lorry

Two of Radio Forth's Easter Bunnies brighten up the Spring scene.

arrived at the Forth Road Bridge — all the bright ribbons were torn off by high winds and the balloons floated off across the Forth leaving a sadly denuded haggis, drenched by torrential rain. The haggis lorry spent a day touring Fife and made for Stirling University where it was to spend the night in the car park before continuing its promotional tour.

During the night some pranksters stole the lorry and set off with it along the A9. They were caught in a snowstorm and simply abandoned the lorry in the middle of the road. Early in the morning Radio Forth received an irate call from the police asking them if they owned the lorry which was blocking the main road in a snowstorm and creating a tailback of traffic.

Tom Steele found himself with the unenviable task of sorting out the problem: "When I 'phoned a motoring organisation to ask them to tow the lorry out of the way, they hung up on me," he said. "I don't blame them for thinking it was a crank telling them he had a lorry with a haggis on top stranded on the A9!"

The lorry was finally brought home and the haggis quietly disposed of. As Burns so rightly said:

The best laid schemes o' mice and Men,
  Gang aft agley,
An' lea'e us nought but grief an' pain,
  For promis'd joy.

Despite the first promotional slip-up, new ideas kept coming forward and many have become firmly established in the Forth Country calendar.

At Easter there are the Radio Forth bunnies. On the Saturday before Easter members of staff are persuaded to climb into bunny costumes — not the silky revealing variety but cover-up woolly costumes with floppy ears. They board the 'bunny buses' with their helpers and boxes of chocolate easter eggs and begin a day-long tour of Edinburgh, Fife, the Lothians and Central Region.

Each bus heads in a different direction and their destinations are broadcast so that children can meet up with them and swap daffodils for easter eggs. At the end of the day the flowers are distributed to hospitals throughout the area.

This exercise has led to one or two hilarious incidents. Mike Scott was travelling along a lonely Fife road in a beach buggy, dressed in his bunny costume, and planning to rendezvous with the bunny bus. Suddenly, his buggy stopped — he had run out of petrol. He had no alternative but to stand by the road side — resplendent in bunny costume — and try to flag down a passing motorist. Understandably, there was some reluctance on the part of drivers to stop for the large bunny. However, he will always be grateful to the attractive girl in the sleek sports car.

On another occasion the bunny bus was twenty minutes ahead of schedule and it was decided to stop at a pub for a drink. There was some consternation on the part of regulars when several life-size bunnies walked in and ordered pints. A new variation on the pink elephant theme!

Large crowds always turn out for the bunny buses and only once has there been any trouble. The GREEN bunny bus arrived at Leith Links just as an ORANGE parade marched past. The orangemen were not impressed by the green bus and the bunnies had to face a barrage of abuse.

Joan Hamilton has been the station's publicity manager for the past six years and, among her responsibilities is the Miss Radio Forth contest. The contest could lead to the Miss World title as the winner progresses from Miss Radio Forth to Miss Scotland, to Miss UK, to Miss World. Joan is keeping her fingers crossed that one girl will actually make that progression one year.

A Radio Forth team make their own music. On guitar Tom Bell, Jay Crawford and Robin Brock, Sandy Wilkie on drums and Ken Haynes on keyboard.

Forth are particularly proud of the teams of school-children which have represented the station on the "What's Happening" children's television series. The children have to answer current affairs questions and the Radio Forth team was runner-up in 1983 and in 1984 they won the title.

Joan and husband, Steve Hamilton (yes, they met at the radio station), coach the youngsters and chaperone them on their exciting trips to the Birmingham television studios. Credit must go to Joan who spends hours scanning the newspapers and even takes the precaution of having the English editions delivered to ensure that nothing is overlooked.

Other promotional ideas over the years have included a custom car show at Ingliston, disco-dancing championships, art competitions, pancake races on Shrove Tuesday and the housewives' roadshow with cookery demonstrations and fashion shows.

Hazel Fowlie conducts an interview from the Navy's Open Day at Rosyth.

CHARITY AUCTION

Another yearly event which creates excitement and frenzied activity in the station is the charity auction which takes place during a weekend before Christmas. All programming is given over to the auctioning of goods donated by businesses and individuals. The money raised buys equipment needed for the care of sick children.

The auction began in 1980 with a target of £12,000 which it met and topped. The following year £32,000 was raised and the figure has been rising ever since. In 1981 a visit from the Bee Gees coincided with the auction and they generously handed over £7,500. They were particularly interested in the fact that the money was being raised to buy equipment for premature babies as one of them had experienced this problem in his own family.

Joan Hamilton explains the logistical problems behind the hugely successful auction: "Over 1,000 businesses have to be circulated to find out if they will take part. All the lot numbers have to be noted and cross-referenced under who donated the item and when it was mentioned on air. People turn up to collect the item they have bid for, often with no idea of the lot number!

"We need 25 people on duty at all times between 10.00 a.m. and 10.00 p.m. on Friday, 8.00 a.m. and 10.00 p.m. on Saturday and 8.30 a.m. until 8.00 p.m. on

Alec Shuttleworth in action, washing a listener's car to raise money for the Charity Auction. Steve Hamilton provides encouragement.

The team answering listener's calls during the Charity Auction.

Sunday to handle the auction. It may sound like a simple exercise but, in fact, it is immensely complicated and takes a great deal of organisation."

Tom Steele's office is piled high with donations — toys, sweets, bicycles, television sets, clothes and boxes of food and drinks.

A large amount of money is raised by the 'pledges'. Listeners make a request for a record and pay up when their request is fulfilled. A surprising number seem to want to hear the presenters sing. So far no Placido Domingo has been discovered on the staff. It is a hectic and nerve-wracking time but everyone at Forth enjoys taking part and is willing to carry out requests — no matter how bizarre. Alec Shuttleworth found himself washing a listener's car in Forth Street — and managed to lock the luckless owner out of his vehicle. Perhaps to discourage further requests for car washes. Bobby Malcolm had to clean the Radio Forth steps with an electric toothbrush and Margo MacDonald was asked to sing *There will always be an England*. Another caller offered money if Margo would sing *Scotland the Brave* but that offer was topped by someone who wanted her to refrain from singing *Scotland the Brave*.

Goods are usually bought for well above their cash value because listeners know that the money is being raised for charity. There are normally about 1,000 items in the auction and, coming as it does just before Christmas, it is an excellent way of buying presents. There is usually one item in the auction which creates special interest. Last year it was a telephone box which now stands in a carpet showroom. The proud new owner paid £1,300 for his acquisition.

Donations from celebrities also bring in high bids. Rod Stewart's satin stage trousers were bought for over £200 and a good price was raised by a set of cartoons drawn by Rolf Harris.

NEW TALENT

Radio Forth is always eager to encourage new talent and a number of awards are presented annually to musicians, writers and sportsmen.

A highlight of the Accordion Shows which are staged each year is the presentation of the awards for Best New Fiddle Tune — the Jimmy McFarlane Memorial Cup — and Best New Accordion Tune — the Jimmy Shand Accordion Trophy. The young composers perform their music for the capacity audience which always turns out for the popular Accordion Shows.

The first was held in 1976 and Sandy Wilkie, now programme co-ordinator at Radio Forth, has been responsible for staging the show over the last few years. The exercise has caused him a few hair-raising moments.

In 1982, as the cast rehearsed in the Playhouse Theatre, all the lights went out. It was 10.30 a.m. and the curtain was due to rise on a full house at 7.30 p.m. Sandy had a difficult decision to make: "Do I cancel the show or hope that things will be sorted out by 7.30 p.m.?"

The old maxim — the show must go on — prevailed and the cast rehearsed with emergency lighting while electricians worked to put right damage caused by water and to restore power to the theatre. The work was completed at 7.20 p.m. and the audience sat back to enjoy the show, knowing nothing of the panic backstage.

Two other musical awards are presented during the Edinburgh Festival. Judges visit all the musical shows on the Fringe and decide on the Best Original Music and the Best Musical Performance.

One young Edinburgh musician who has shown considerable talent is teenager Tommy Smith of Wester Hailes. He won a coveted scholarship to the world's top jazz college in Boston, USA but needed an extra £6,000 before he could take up the offer. Forth contributed £1,000 to the fund which managed to raise the money and Tommy should have a brilliant career ahead of him which Radio Forth will watch with interest.

The Radio Forth Youth Orchestra was formed in 1979 and gave its first public performance in the Queen's Hall in June, 1980. The orchestra was created to give young musicians in the 13-18 age group the opportunity to perform in a professional concert hall. They also experienced recording conditions as the programme is broadcast on Radio Forth. The youngsters put on a spring and winter concert and achieve remarkably high standards. Many of them have gone on to become professionals.

Writing talent receives its reward with the short story competition held during the Edinburgh Festival. Listeners submit scripts which are read by a panel of judges and the winners receive awards plus the opportunity to hear their stories read on Radio Forth. Leslie Thomas presented the prizes in 1983, Peter Ustinov did the honours in 1984 and Radio Forth has now linked up with the Trustee Savings Bank to further enhance the prize value of the competition.

New comedy-writing talent was encouraged to come forward with the "Six of the Best" series promoted by Radio Forth, Radio Clyde and STV. Six half-hour comedy scripts were selected from the hundreds submitted and were produced on radio.

A line-up of some of the talented young musicians who have played in the Radio Forth Youth Orchestra.

There have been art competitions for children and a craft competition — the winners had their work displayed at the Churchill Theatre.

There have been yachting trophies, canoeing trophies, a cycling contest, a majorette competition — you name it and Radio Forth will have found a way of involving itself in the many and varied activities of the people in this area.

The majorettes who won the Radio Forth competition caused something of a problem in the Festival Cavalcade — the parade which opens the Edinburgh

Festival each year. It takes at least two hours for the long procession of floats to make their way from Regent Terrace, along Princes Street to the Grassmarket and it took even longer when the Radio Forth majorettes took part. Their march pattern of two steps forward and three back created quite a hold-up!

Bobby Malcolm　　Radio Forth

Dick Barrie　　Radio Forth

Hazel Fowlie　　Radio Forth

Tom Bell　　Radio Fo

Ken Haynes Radio Forth

Bill Barclay Radio

MIKE SCOTT

Judi White

Graham Jackson

bin Brock   Radio Forth

Steve Jack   Radio Forth

rk Hagen   Radio Forth

David Scott

POP AND . . .

One comment guaranteed to enrage the staff of Radio Forth is: "It's nothing but pop, isn't it?"

Yes, pop plays a large part in the station's output. The public have made it clear that they want a strong emphasis on music in their daytime listening. Forth does not dictate public taste — it responds to public demand. A commercial organisation has no other choice for it must pay its bills and the only way to do that is to attract advertising. Advertisers will only use the medium if they can be persuaded that a lot of people are listening — and people will only listen if they WANT to listen.

However, the suggestion that Radio Forth is "nothing but pop" is outrageously inaccurate. The station puts out serious, in-depth documentaries, discussion programmes, a nightly half-hour news magazine plus the regular news bulletins. There are weekly in-depth programmes covering all the topics which are of current concern, such as drug abuse, glue sniffing, unemployment, the National Health Service, housing, and so on.

There are lighter speech programmes on ever-popular topics such as gardening, holidays, beauty care, fashion, fishing, photography — the list is endless. All the mysteries of the computer, for example, were unlocked in the series *Poke of Chips*.

During the day the music is interspersed by inter-

John Shedden and Gwyneth Guthrie record the Mary Queen of Scots series, the first drama to be produced by an ILR station.

views with guests, many of whom are experts offering advice and answering listeners' queries. We have had the Radio Forth doctor, the dentist, the vet, the keep-fit expert, the do-it-yourself expert, the financial wizard and wine connoisseur.

Books and Batons is the popular book, classical music and arts programme produced by Ruth Morrison. Ruth also organises literary lunches — a ticket buys you a good meal and an opportunity to hear a talk from someone well-known in the literary world.

Radio Forth has broadcast many award-winning documentaries including *The Big Hoose* which was an inside look at life for prisoners in Saughton Jail, Edinburgh.

Bill Barclay has entertained the prisoners on several occasions and he, with the help of David Johnston, was given the 'freedom' of the prison to talk to anyone from guards to lifers. The prisoners are avid fans of Forth and often send in requests for their families.

In September, 1982 Margo MacDonald tackled the difficult issue of drugs on the Forth Forum programme and the result was another award and widespread praise. She exposed a situation which had been cloaked in secrecy but which, since then, has been well covered in other media. The programme featured interviews with drug addicts, some of whom admitted to peddling drugs to raise money to buy their own supplies.

A newspaper commented at the time: "Radio Forth is to be congratulated on what has been quite simply the most important social document I have heard on radio ... conscience stirring, physically frightening and almost sick-making. I have already discovered that it has been most unpopular among the supply section of the local drugs industry." The Scottish Office asked for a recording of the programme and Government concern about the problem was quickly expressed together with new funding to combat the problem.

Radio Forth organised a nuclear debate, chaired by Richard Findlay, in the Playhouse Theatre and there was a packed house of 3,000 people to listen to and debate with politicians, academics and other interested parties. A debate on education was also arranged so that ratepayers could put their views on current cuts in public spending on the vital education services.

Election time is fairly hectic for the news and features department as they arrange discussion programmes and coverage of the election results. The competition to be first with the results is always fierce. Local radio has an advantage over all other media as it can bring the local news to listeners as it happens.

Six weeks before the June election in 1983 Radio Forth ran a telephone poll which revealed that 23 per cent of the voters in their area had not made up their minds which party to support but it indicated how many votes each party could expect and proved to be remarkably accurate when the result of the election was known. Another pre-election programme was a mock election at Dunfermline High School which gave pupils the opportunity to play politics.

Special campaign weeks are organised to highlight particular subjects — it could be fire prevention, numeracy, the law, social security, road safety or health.

The anti-smoking campaign brings back painful memories for most of the Radio Forth staff. The pressures of broadcasting often lead to chain-smoking habits and only reluctantly did all the smokers agree to a no-smoking week. Many made it through the week with the aid of pea pods as replacement cigarettes or worry beads to occupy restless hands. An award from ASH (the anti-smoking organisation) hangs proudly in Tom Steele's office but you can scarcely see the award for the pall of smoke!

One very successful campaign was 'For Your Benefit Week'. A team from the Department of Health and Social Security manned the special 'phone lines which are put in for the campaign weeks and discovered that one in six of the callers they dealt with did not know what they were entitled to in social benefits. They dealt with 500 calls in four days.

Another interesting exercise was the Young Scot project. A handy booklet was printed containing all the information a young school-leaver needs — where to

The football crowd spectate while Bill Barclay makes a spectacle of himself.

look for advice on job-hunting, or any other topic, where sporting facilities are available, where to find entertainment and a host of other facts and figures.

Pop singer and songwriter, B.A. Robertson, presented a series of two-minute features. The idea has been taken up on the Continent and Tom Steele was in Germany last December to explain how the scheme worked.

Forth Action is another example of the radio station's links with the community. It was launched in August 1980 and provides information and support to organisations in the area which want to use Radio Forth to promote their work. Two Community Service Volunteers run the unit and bring the volunteers and those needing their help together.

Another service to listeners is Forthbeat which is organised by Judi White. She receives information on fund-raising activities in Forth Country and ensures that air-time is given to all of them.

Margo MacDonald jokingly refers to herself as "long-words editor" and she is involved in many of the broadcasts covering serious topics. However, she is probably best known for her Sunday morning *Dial Margo* series. The "phone-in" programme is a minefield for any broadcaster as no-one knows what to expect from the next call. There is a delay button to cut off any obscenities or anything illegal but Margo is proud of the fact that she has never had to use it: "I think it would sound odd to other listeners if a caller was suddenly cut off — they would wonder what was being censored," she explains. "I always warn people if I think they are on dangerous ground and explain that they musn't name names. Very few people are rude and any swearing has been pretty inoffensive."

Margo has strong opinions on most topics but she knows that her point of view is not what the programme is about. The listeners put their points of view and she has the delicate task of playing devil's advocate.

Dial Margo is an important platform for listeners to express their opinions and it provides a link between the public and the people in power.

Many people have had problems solved by airing their grievance on the programme. There was the student who was told he could not have his grant because his application had been lost in the post. Someone in authority heard him ask Margo for advice and immediately sorted out his problem.

On another occasion Margo noticed that new budget arrangements would mean VAT on Meals on Wheels. Edinburgh MP James Douglas-Hamilton 'phoned her to say that he would be taking the matter up immediately.

The Radio Forth news team race to meet their deadline.

The hourly news bulletins which go out during the day are prepared by News Editor, David Johnston, and his team of reporters.

Each weekday evening, from 5.30 p.m. until 6.00 p.m., there is the news magazine programme *Forth Report* when listeners can catch up on local, national and international news and hear interviews with the people who are in the news.

Sport is a top priority at Forth and Vic Wood is the man in charge of the sports team. He talks about sports coverage now and in the past: "Ten years of sport on Radio Forth has been an eye-opener and an excellent education for those supporters and active members who have watched the fluctuation of football teams in

Forth Country and seen the rapid development of personal participation. Trends have changed very quickly on the recreation and leisure front. It is difficult to believe that there was scarcely a jogger on the city routes and the country lanes just a decade ago.

"Those faithful followers of sport on Forth will recognise the changes over the years but I will throw in a few memorable names from the early years. Do you remember George Farm, the one-time Blackpool and Hibs goalkeeper who guided Dunfermline into European football and who caused a mini-riot every Saturday at lunchtimes with his caustic comments on the local scene?

"Do you remember the jovial 17-stone John McLaren whose jaunty air and rapier-like wit softened the barbs of George Farm or the machine-gun voice of George Barton who provided much of the sports result service on Saturdays?

"I wonder too how many listened to the humour of Iain Agnew in the early days when he filled in with his hilarious talents before changing his style and his allegiance to STV and *Take the High Road*?

"Did you know that gamekeeper Bob Taylor was one of the original Sportsbeat presenters?

"So, that's the sports quiz over. I am more qualified to talk about Radio Forth sport from 1976-78 and then 1980-85. Bill Greig (now with the Daily Express) was one of my predecessors. So was Kim Sabido who features prominently on ITN news bulletins.

"But really, sport on Radio Forth has taken off with a 'Kick Into the Eighties' and I'm glad to say that I have been ably supported by such professionals as Donald Ford and Alan Gordon over these past vital years.

"Presenters have been Tom Bell and Bill Barclay but we have gone full circle again for our main Saturday Sportsbeat with Tom Bell and myself hosting the programme from 3.00 p.m. until 6.00 p.m. and the most

Sports team Vic Wood, Tom Bell and Donald Ford. (left to right)

exciting development means that Donald Ford and Alan Gordon are out and about bringing live second-half commentary from one of the major football matches in Scotland.

"But the lads are perhaps the known names. I am

lucky enough to have a vast part-time 'army' of corres-
pondents throughout the land and it is our proud boast
that we average 23 different sports each Saturday.

"If you want to keep in touch with sport in Forth
Country, we have a midweek Sportsbeat on Wednesday nights from 8.00 p.m. and a weekend sports pre-
view every Friday from 6.00 p.m. through until 6.30
p.m.

"Whether it is Alan Gordon and myself on senior
football, we have Andy Balfour scouring the junior
grades, excellent rugby reporters in Peter Donald and
Bernie Lodge plus badminton, squash, stock car rac-
ing, horse-racing and even flounder-tramping from
the Solway if Bill Hill remembers!

"I am proud to have such a team to captain. I am
proud that our sports programmes ARE sports programmes and not entirely soccer. As we celebrate our
10th birthday, we have lots of reminiscences. By the
time we've reached our 11th birthday, we shall have
even more to celebrate in sporting terms."

BEHIND THE SCENES

A visit behind the scenes of any operation is always fascinating and an eye-opener. Radio Forth shows hundreds of visitors around its studios and many are surprised to discover just how complex is a disc jockey's life. Anyone's job looks easy if it is done well and professionally but there is usually more to it than is immediately obvious.

Presenters have to arrive at Radio Forth long before they are 'on-air'. They select their records from the library which has 40,000 singles, 15,500 popular albums and 2,000 classical albums. As a guide they have a playlist which is compiled each week by the Head of Music. He works with current charts plus his own knowledge of what is new and what is likely to be popular. He also has research on the music which is selling best in Forth Country.

The features department provides the material for the various speech inserts in the programmes.

On music policy, the Radio Forth watchword is 'melody'. The *Voice Your Choice* programme gives listeners the opportunity to request the music they want and the choice of records is carefully noted by presenters when they compile their own programmes.

The disc jockey has to keep a log of all the music played and he is responsible for cueing the records, commercials and regular information spots — not to mention ensuring that everything winds up neatly on time for the News on the hour.

Engineer Graham Warman takes a breather on top of the Radio Forth landrover.

There is a constant stream of information coming at him on road conditions, weather, travel etc. and when a guest comes in the presenter must find time to put him or her at ease. Throughout all this activity he has to keep up his friendly chat with the most important people of all — the listeners.

When the programme is over it is time to prepare the next day's material and there will be other demands on the disc jockey's off-duty time — opening sales of work, judging competitions and giving talks about the radio station.

As you will gather, a presenter's job is more complex than it sounds but, of course, there is an engineer in the background to ensure that the equipment works and everthing goes smoothly. Chief Engineer, Ian Wales, has five engineers working for him and they have various studios to look after plus master control, two news booths, a 22 foot outside broadcast unit, radio cars plus a Kirkcaldy studio. Ian estimates that around 5,000 miles of tape are used each year. IBA engineers visit the station once a year to check that the equipment is in good working order and up to the high standards expected.

Outside broadcasts offer a challenge to the engineers and one of the most difficult was the Pope's visit when Ian Wales had to stretch his resources almost to the limit to cover all the Pope's stopping-off points. There was tight security everywhere and everything had to be meticulously planned in advance. One major snag developed when it was discovered that the reporter who was to cover the Pope's arrival at Cardinal Gray's residence had not turned up and he had in his possession the security passes. Margo dashed up to the location at Morningside and, because she was recognised by the police, she was allowed into the commentary position.

There are regular outside broadcasts throughout the

year from the Youth Orchestra concerts, the Accordion shows, football and other sporting activities plus special occasions such as Navy Day at Rosyth.

"One of the most unusual outside broadcasts was from the Goodyear airship," says Ian. "One I felt I had to do myself was from on board the training ship, the "Malcolm Miller" which had an all-girl crew! On that occasion I was on my way out to the ship when I discovered I had forgotten the transmission aerial."

What a radio station wants to avoid at all costs is silence on the airwaves and breakdowns leading to this disaster have been surprisingly few. Ian remembers the night the radio station was off the air for six minutes — an eternity in broadcasting time: "The emergency generator which we switch to if the power fails let us down on this occasion but that was the only time it did," he said. "Sometimes there will be a bad line on an outside broadcast but we have plenty of contingency arrangements for coping when things go wrong."

The Radio Forth sales team are a vital element in the radio station's structure. They must persuade advertisers to spend their money and the more money they bring in, the better the service Forth can offer.

Sales Manager, George Wilson, explains: "We have to bring in enough money to pay the rental to the IBA, tax, rates, salaries, dividends to shareholders, broadcasting equipment — it's a long list and a heavy bill. Every salesman has his product to sell to the customer — our product is the programming. Advertisers can buy their specific spot in the programmes they want or 'pick and mix' as they please — and their adverts become part of the programme, informing about their goods and services, sometimes bringing in a touch of humour or a catchy jingle."

One quarter of all the commercials are actually made in Radio Forth's studios by the commercial production

Sales and marketing manager, George Wilson.

team. There are checks on adverts to ensure that they do not infringe the strict guidelines laid down. As well as the checks on sound and advertising quality, the IBA keeps a close watch on programmes. The programme schedules have to be submitted to London for approval and there are local watchdogs only too eager to point out any slip-ups.

Then there are the AUDIENCE RESEARCH FIGURES. Everyone in the station quakes a little when the figures are announced for the statistics will be thoroughly examined to find out just where listeners are being won and lost. Each presenter hopes to see his share of the listeners increased, the news team want to see large audiences for their bulletins and nightly news magazine, while the features department, like everyone else, anxiously scans the important percentages.

The surveys are carried out on a large sample of people in the area covered by the station. The listeners are cross-examined about their listening habits and the results give the broadcasters some idea of the percentage of the population tuning in to different programmes.

The Independent Broadcasting Authority conducts research too and have come up with some interesting views from the people of Forth Country. With the permission of the IBA, we have reproduced some of the tables from their 1984 research.

Listening experience of Radio Forth
In numbers of regular and weekly listeners, Radio Forth and Radio 1 were the two most popular stations, easily ahead of all the competing services:

	Heard of	Ever listened	Listen regularly	Listened: in past week	yesterday
	%	%	%	%	%
Radio Forth	99	89	44	43	31
BBC Radio 1	98	74	41	38	29
BBC Radio 2	93	60	23	22	16
BBC Radio Scotland	94	60	19	18	11
BBC Radio 4	82	33	11	12	9
BBC Radio 3	81	27	5	5	3
Radio Luxembourg	93	52	5	4	2
Radio Clyde (Glasgow)	80	32	4	4	1
Radio Tay (Dundee/Perth)	59	14	*	*	*

(* = less than 0.5%)

Station choice for satisfying listener requirements
The following table shows the proportion of these listeners who said they tuned into the radio for each type of output and went on to nominate various stations as being "very good" at providing it. Thus, for example, of the 426 listeners (71% of the sample of 601) who used the radio for background music, 38% thought BBC Radio 1 to be a very good source of this, 35% thought Radio Forth to be very good, and so on.

| | | Per cent saying "very good" | | | | |
	Base	*R Forth*	*R1*	*R2*	*R Scot*	*R4*
Background music	(426)%	35	38	22	8	1
Things to make one cheerful	(402)%	41	37	18	11	4
World and UK news	(395)%	32	24	15	20	15
Phone-in programmes	(344)%	64	11	8	11	6
Concentrating on music	(338)%	30	32	18	10	6
Presenters' personalities	(327)%	37	31	21	13	5
Local information	(324)%	85	3	1	8	*
Scottish news	(313)%	52	6	4	35	4
Non-musical entertainment	(258)%	34	21	11	17	21
Sports coverage	(230)%	33	9	20	30	5
Current affairs etc.	(190)%	27	9	12	24	29
To feel part of community	(151)%	77	3	1	6	*

(* = less than 0.5%)

Radio Forth's effectiveness in meeting audience requirements
The above table illustrates Radio Forth's standing among different sections of the radio audience, when segmented according to their stated listening requirements. Forth emerged as the 'first choice' station for nine of the twelve listed aspects of radio output. It ranks second in the three other categories.

Station choice at breakfast-time

Respondents who said they ever listened to the radio at this time of day were asked which station they most often tuned to, and whether there were other stations they sometimes listened to at breakfast-time. Results were as follows:

	Listened to most often %	Ever listen to %
Radio Forth	32	43
BBC Radio 1	28	39
BBC Radio Scotland	15	24
BBC Radio 2	15	22
BBC Radio 4	7	10
BBC Radio 3	1	2

Thus, Radio Forth emerged as the most listened-to station at this daily peak listening time. Asked about reasons for their choice of station at this time of day, those preferring Radio Forth emphasised their liking for the local news and information, the music, traffic news and the cheerful, friendly presenter. BBC Radio 1 tended to be chosen for the music played and the presenter.

Because of the difficulties in identifying a radio audience and whether or not it is satisfied with programmes, the programme-makers love to hear from their listeners.

Competition for the ear of the public is fierce. More leisure time means more opportunity for everyone in the entertainment industry and it is a field which is

Jay Crawford's afternoon programme coming live from the Radio Forth Outside Broadcast caravan at the Ideal Homes Exhibition, Ingliston.

constantly changing as public demand changes. There are always those who can't understand why a well-loved feature or presenter is dropped. But think how moribund radio would become if nothing ever changed.

Radio Forth was an infant on the radio scene ten years ago. Now it can claim a wealth of experience and many well-known broadcasters have learned their trade on the station which is a natural nursery for new talent. Demo tapes are frequently sent in by would-be broadcasters and all are carefully listened to in order to ensure that no new talent is overlooked.

CLANGERS AND RED FACES

As you might expect, things do not always go smooth-ly in a radio station. People are caught off-balance or equipment breaks down, leaving the broadcaster with egg on his face.

Getting your words in a fankle is an obvious danger and newsreader, Harry Smith (now with BBC TV) once introduced the news with: "This is Radio Smith, Harry Forth reporting."

On another occasion, news girl Margaret Vaughan was alone in the news booth reading the last news bulletin of the night when she felt something on her foot. To her horror she saw a small brown mouse staring up at her, perched on her shoe. Margaret bravely continued with the news but, the instant she was off-air, she let out an anguished scream for help.

The radio station found itself involved with an agor-aphobic elephant at Edinburgh Zoo. Eleven year old Dali had arrived in Edinburgh from Whipsnade Zoo and for three years had refused to place more than her head and two front legs outside her shelter. Hypnotism and valium had been tried but nothing could persuade Dali to venture further. Disc jockeys visited the Zoo and offered all sorts of temptations from crisps and buns to chocolate biscuits but the elephant refused to budge. As Jay Crawford began his live broadcast from Dali's enclosure she showed her disapproval by blowing soil in his face.

She was equally unimpressed by the persuasive talents of Micky Dolenz, one-time singer with the Monkees, who called on the shy elephant during a visit to Edinburgh.

Eventually, all attempts were abandoned. It was discovered some years later that Dali had been refusing to trespass on the territory of her next-door neighbour, the elephant Sally. When Sally died, Dali emerged at last from her self-imposed incarceration. It was not agoraphobia she had been suffering from — she had been following her tribal instincts.

Forth's oddest fans were a battery of hens terrified by thunder and lightning. The owner of the hens 'phoned the station to congratulate them on calming his panicking brood. The storm had caused panic in the battery and, when battening down all the hatches and turning on the lights failed to calm the hens, the radio was switched on. The sound of Radio Forth quietened the frightened chicks.

On one occasion a ghost interfered with a tape-recorder which reporter, Ninian Reid, was using for his *Walkabout Forth Country* series. He was being shown round an old inn which was reputedly haunted by its first landlady. Ninian's tape-recorder worked perfectly before he entered the haunted house and there were no problems when he emerged but the machine would not operate inside the hostelry.

Ninian had another embarrassing experience as he finished off his lunchtime snack in the studio just before the red light for the one o'clock news came on. He had just taken a mouthful of juice when he realised, to his horror, that he was on. Shock caused him to spray his carefully-typed news script with juice. It was a credit to Ninian's sang-froid that he continued to read the spattered news script without faltering while all around him collapsed in silent laughter.

Laughter on air is always a problem — at least

Jay Crawford

controlling it is. Bill Torrance had problems when his guest, Calum Kennedy, disappeared below the table during an interview — his seat had collapsed under him.

Jay Crawford had an even bigger problem when a guest — 'tired and emotional' — fell fast asleep in the studio in the middle of an interview.

Selecting an appropriate record to play when a celebrity dies poses its own problems. When news of Bing Crosby's death was announced the unfortunate disc jockey played one of the singer's best-loved numbers — *Dancing Cheek to Cheek*. It starts with the line "Heaven, I'm in Heaven . . ."

Mike Scott and Sandy Wilkie will never forget the morning they were to rendezvous with the Royal Navy aircraft carrier, *Hermes*, for an outside broadcast — and were very nearly arrested. The Breakfast Show was to come from the ship as it sailed up the Forth. Sandy and Mike arrived at North Berwick harbour at 3.00 a.m. on a Friday morning. A cold mist hung eerily over the Forth. They searched the dark waters for some sign of the dinghy which would take them out to the *Hermes* and began to worry as the deadline for the show drew nearer and no dinghy appeared. Suddenly a police car drew up alongside them and two police-men demanded to know what they were doing hang-ing about the harbour at such an hour.

"When I told them we were waiting for an aircraft carrier it was obvious that they thought they had a pair of lunatics on their hands," said Sandy.

"However, they finally accepted our story and just at that moment we spotted the dinghy through the mist. It was heading towards Dunbar instead of North Ber-wick. The policemen saved the situation by flashing a message to the sailors with their torches and directing the dinghy to the harbour.

"A gust of wind whipped one of the policemen's hats off into the Forth. I often wondered how he explained his missing hat when he got back to base."

The broadcast, you will be glad to hear, went without a hitch.

One of the worst moments for the station occurred in the early days when Tom Bell, presenting an evening programme, became aware that his feet were damp. He alerted the rest of the staff who discovered water gushing from a 3″ pipe which carried mains water. The water was coming with such force that soon the base-ment was 4″ deep in water and, once the pipe was repaired, there was a big mopping-up operation. It was a miracle that the water had not come in contact with

Presenter Bob Malcolm with Telly Savalas.

powerful electric cables in the building as that would have caused thousands of pounds worth of damage. Dehumidifiers were brought in to dry out the carpets.

There have been problems with unruly guests — notably one pop group who arrived for an interview very drunk and proceeded to create havoc, smashing the coffee machine and the fire alarm. Their record company paid for the damage but they were not thereafter made welcome at Forth.

"Most of our guests are charming and they were very much the exception," said Sandy.

One perk for the staff of a radio station is meeting the famous personalities who call in to promote their

Charlton Heston and Clarke Tait chat about the star's life-story.

latest record, book, film or whatever. Sophia Loren, Charlton Heston, Peter Ustinov, Stewart Granger, Elton John, Cliff Richard and Telly Savalas are just a few of the big names who have signed the visitors' book at the reception desk.

Forth has also had its royal contacts and Bob Malcolm, Jay Crawford and Steve Jack attended a reception at Buckingham Palace hosted by the Queen. The first royal interview on commercial radio in the UK was on Radio Forth when Richard Findlay interviewed the Duke of Edinburgh at Holyrood Palace in 1975.

FESTIVAL CITY RADIO

Forth's latest achievement was another broadcasting first. Festival City Radio was launched on August 12th, 1984 and ran for the three weeks of the Edinburgh Festival.

On VHF 96.8 listeners could tune into four programme segments during the day when guests chatted about their productions in the Festival, reviewers discussed performances and excerpts from shows were broadcast.

Meanwhile, on medium wave, the normal, familiar popular format continued.

This made history for independent local radio. Permission had been obtained from the Home Office and the IBA for this experiment and all eyes were on Edinburgh to see how the project worked. Sponsorship was allowed for the first time but Richard Findlay promised, at a pre-launch reception: "It will not be the type of sponsorship you may have heard in America — we intend to do things much more tastefully as behoves the fine traditions of British broadcasting." The sponsors taking part in this historic landmark were British Airways.

Alec Shuttleworth and Jenny Brown hosted the morning programme, Clive Sandground the lunchtime show, Dolina MacLennan and Sandy Nielsen the evening show, and Mike Maran was the host for the late-night programme.

Alec Shuttleworth

In past years Radio Forth had run a Festival City Radio programme covering Festival events and Tom Steele hit on the idea of running a separate radio station on the VHF frequency. He said: "We wondered if we could get the necessary permission from the Home Office and the IBA and were delighted when we were given the go-ahead. The next problem Richard had was finding a sponsor to pay for the venture. There wasn't much response from Scottish companies but Saatchi and Saatchi snapped up the idea for British Airways."

On July 23rd Richard Findlay received the news that the money was agreed and everything could go ahead.

Tom was holidaying in the tiny village of Borrodale in the south of Harris when he received a call from Richard.

"I was thrilled when I got the message that Festival City Radio could go ahead," he said. "But we had to get everything together before August 12th — just three weeks in which to find the staff, work out the schedules, fix up interviews and guests. It was a daunting prospect."

The reception to launch Festival City Radio was followed by a Scottish show in the Playhouse Theatre and the presenters, producers — everybody involved in the new venture — knew that they had a busy time ahead.

A highlight for everyone was the broadcasting of the Fireworks Concert which is now established as a spectacular Edinburgh Festival event. Glenlivet sponsor the concert by the Scottish Chamber Orchestra in the Ross Bandstand in Princes Street Gardens and Handel's Fireworks music is accompanied by a fabulous fireworks display from the Castle. Radio Forth broadcast the concert for those viewing the fireworks but out-of-earshot of the music. The crowds in Princes Street were listening eagerly to transistors — a heartening sight for a radio man who does not normally see his audience.

Festival City Radio was a boon to visitors and local people for it provided information about the Festival along with interviews with the famous and not-so-famous, and an opportunity to air controversial topics. It was appropriate that the experiment should have coincided with the new Labour District Council's protestation that the Festival was elitist and only for the middle class. Radio Forth brought the Festival into every home, regardless of class.

It also gave Richard the idea of expanding the Radio Forth operation. He puts it this way: "There is the

Radio Forth's new premises in Kirkcaldy's High Street which house a shop and a studio.

possibility of running different programmes permanently on VHF but funding is the problem. It is difficult enough sustaining one station on our budget. However, Festival City Radio has allowed us to find out what problems we would face and has given us the opportunity to gauge reaction from listeners to a lot of speech radio.

"We also enjoyed the challenge, even if it was exhausting. Don't forget, we also ran Radio Forth at the same time for those whose taste did not run to Festival material."

THE NEXT DECADE

The tenth birthday is a time for looking back but, more important, for looking to the future.

Radio Forth's franchise has just been renewed so that the company can look forward with confidence, knowing that the IBA is happy with their efforts so far. However, it is not a station that will complacently sit back and rest on its laurels.

One of the biggest plans for the future is a change of venue. The building in Forth Street creates major problems. It is a Georgian building — hardly designed to meet the needs of a modern commercial radio station. The search is on for new premises and Chief Engineer, Ian Wales, has dreams of purpose-built studios: "So much has changed in ten years," he said. "Great strides have been made in radio equipment just as they have in all fields of technology. Our equipment is constantly being up-dated and works very effectively but there are sound problems in a building like this."

In January, 1984 Radio Forth opened a shop and studio in Kirkcaldy's High Street to bring the station closer to its Fife listeners. On occasions live shows come from this studio and it is used to transmit news from Fife as fast as possible. There is also a facility there for booking theatre tickets and, of course, there are plenty of items on display to purchase. The new shop makes it easier for Fife listeners to hand in requests or other communications for the radio station.

Chairman of Radio Forth, Mr Max Harper-Gow at the opening of the Kirckaldy shop and studio. With him is Mr Bob King, Convener of Fife Regional Council.

Tom Steele sees it this way: "A radio station is about people. Radio Forth is not a transmitter, turntable, discs, tape recorders and electronic wizardry. That form of definition is similar to describing your closest friend as a pair of jeans and a T-shirt. That is the apparel . . . Radio Forth is the voices and the personalities of those behind the microphone whether they belong to our own talented broadcast team or those we introduce to our listeners.

"We are the shop window and a mirror, a reflection and a showcase of the local way of life. A way of life that is unique because of where it is. Therefore our programming policy and its future is linked to East Central Scotland. We call it Forth Country. It's a form of togetherness."

Richard is also Chairman of the Association of Independent Radio Contractors (AIRC) and this gives him an excellent perspective on the future of radio. The organisation represents the 47 independent stations across the country and is constantly looking at future prospects for the industry.

Richard says: "We think it is time to look carefully at sound broadcasting so that we have, at once, both a diverse yet a cohesive pattern and all listeners are catered for with top quality programmes. I like to think of our company as not only a local radio station but as a communications organisation. That is why I am interested in the development of cable television, other forms of radio services, local television and broadcast data. Our heart is in our community and if there are other benefits we can bring to it we'll do our best to ensure that we can play a proper part, but only a fool would tear out his roots and ours are firmly in Radio Forth and the hand-in-hand relationship we have with our listeners. We have lots of plans for the future."

Whatever lies ahead, Radio Forth never forgets that the listeners are the VIPs and the station wants to remain CLOSE TO YOU — AND ANYBODY ELSE WHO KNOWS YOU!

AWARDS

Perhaps Radio Forth is entitled to boast a little as they celebrate their tenth birthday.

A radio station can't afford to be a shrinking violet — its job is to get out there and persuade listeners to tune in — so here, with no apologies, is a list of some of the awards received over the years.

1976
Radio Campaign Awards
For Station Promotion — public service announcement (how to find 194 on the dial). Produced by Maggie Dimambro, v/o Bill Torrance and Rose McBain.

1977
U.N.D.A. Awards
Second prize for *View from Earth* at the Seville Festival of Religious Broadcasting sponsored by U.N.D.A., the Roman Catholic International Organisation which encourages new developments in religious broadcasting. Jointly produced by Hazel Fowlie and Father Andrew Monaghan.

1978

Argos Consumer Writer's Award
Winning award in the Broadcasting Section for a 20 minute magazine programme on the Unfair Contract Terms Act which came into legislation that year. Produced by Hazel Fowlie and presented by Maeve Robertson and Iain Agnew.

Imperial Tobacco Awards
Award for Best Scripted Community programme for *View from Earth* dealing with the Lanthorn project in Livingston new town where for the first time in Scotland the four Protestant Churches of the Livingston experiment joined with the Roman Catholic Church and the local authorities in a new type of partnership which resulted in a combined Church-Community centre. Presented by Hazel Fowlie assisted by Radio Forth's religious adviser, Father Andrew Monaghan.

1979

Ash Awards
For services to health education on smoking in Scotland for the year 1979 presented by the Scottish Committee of Action on Smoking and Health. Award received by Hamish Wilson, Features and Special Projects Producer.

U.N.D.A. Awards
First prize at the Seville Festival of Religious Broadcasting for a special edition of *View from Earth* entitled *A Time to Listen*. Produced by Hazel Fowlie and Father Andrew Monaghan.

Radio & Record News and Radio Month Awards for Local Radio

Best Minority Interest Programme for the *View from Earth* special programme dealing with the Lanthorn project.

Best Emergency Programming for *The Snowline* presented by the entire staff of Radio Forth and co-ordinated by The Programme Controller, Tom Steele. Radio Forth provided the only means of communication and instant help during the New Year holiday period when Scotland was devastated by snow storms and Edinburgh ground to a total halt. The situation was compounded by a local authority dispute involving road gritters and Radio Forth opened its airwaves 24 hours a day for three days as a source of help, information and comfort. Teams of volunteer plumbers, drivers and voluntary workers based themselves at the station and formed emergency help squads.

Sandford St. Martin Trust Awards

Local Radio Station Award for best religious output throughout 1979.

Radio Industries Club of Scotland Awards

The Radio Entertainment Award for *McLaughlin's Ceilidh* presented by Jack McLaughlin.

Special Award presented by the *Daily Record* for *Keeper of the Past* produced and presented by Eamonn Hyde.

1980

British Local Radio Awards
Best Local Radio 'Phone-In Award for *The Open Line,*
Saturday late-night problem 'phone-in programme
chaired by Hazel Fowlie. Listeners' problems discussed with experienced panel of counsellors.

ILR Advertising Awards
Certificate of Commendation for Best Station Promo-
tion Announcement awarded for *Recruitment
Wonderwoman* (local sales promotion). Produced and
written by Rod Jones, v/o Rose McBain and Gerry
Sleven.

Radio Industries Club of Scotland Awards
Best Factual Series on Radio award for *The Open Line.*
   Top Radio Personality of the Year won by Bill Torr-
ance.

1981

Radio Industries Club of Scotland Awards
Best Factual Series on Radio award for *The Big Hoose*
— a documentary about Saughton Prison produced by
David Johnston and Bill Barclay and presented by
Richard Findlay.

1982

Radio Industries Club of Scotland Awards
Radio Topicality Award for *Forth Forum* — special
programme dealing with drug abuse, produced and
presented by Margo MacDonald.
   Special award for outstanding contribution for *Six of
the Best* won jointly with Radio Clyde and STV. New
team of comedy writers invited to write six comedy
programmes for radio sponsored by STV.

Steve Hamilton with his Radio Industries Club award for top radio entertainer in 1984 and Mark Hagen with his award for best magazine programme.

1983

International Radio Festival of New York
Award for *The Story of Golf*, written by Clarke Tait, produced and presented by Richard Findlay.

Sony Radio Awards
Best Local Radio Programme Award for *Forth Forum*, produced and presented by Margo MacDonald.

Radio Industries Club of Scotland Awards
Radio Entertainer of the Year won by Steve Hamilton.
  Best Radio Magazine Programme Award for *Monday, Monday* produced and presented by Mark Hagen.
  Highly Commended in the category of Radio Entertainment for *Breaker, Breaker, Music Maker*, C.B. programme presented by Ken Haynes.

*Joan Hamilton with the Radio Forth team, winners of the
1984 Central Television "What's Happening" quiz. Back
row (l to r) Lorna Drummond, Paula Coyle. Front row (l to
r) Stephen Malcolm, Joan Hamilton, Gavin Bostock.*

1984
*International Festival sponsored by the World
Association for Christmas Communication and the
I.C.A. for Radio and Television*
Scottish Award, Category A, Christian Worship, was
won for *Christmas Watchnight Service* produced by
Radio Forth.

Central Television's 'What's Happening' Quiz
This children's television quiz series was won by the
Radio Forth team.

International Radio Festival of New York
Finalist for *Journey To The Centre of the Earth*, a live recording of Rick Wakeham's work by the Edinburgh Secondary School's Orchestra and Chorus together with a rock band, recorded and broadcast by Radio Forth.

DIRECTORS OF THE COMPANY

Chairman: L.M. Harper Gow, MBE. In addition to his Chairmanship of Radio Forth, 'Max' Harper Gow is a director of many other well known Scottish companies, including the Scottish Widows Fund and Life Assurance Society, of which he is a past Chairman, the Royal Bank of Scotland PLC, of which he is a Vice Chairman, Edinburgh Investment Trust PLC, The Scottish Council Development and Industry and Christian Salvesen Ltd. He is Dean of the Consular Corps in Edinburgh/Leith and Honorary Consul for Norway in the city.

Managing Director/Chief Executive: Richard Findlay. Currently also Chairman of the Association of Independent Radio Contractors, having played a wide and varied role in the industry's association over the years. He has been Managing Director of Radio Forth since 1977, is a Director of the Radio Marketing Bureau, the Fruit Market Gallery and a member of the Scottish Community Education Council.

Financial Director/Company Secretary: Alan Wilson. Has been with Radio Forth from the beginning, having worked in television and publishing.

Programme Director: Thomas Steele. Joined Radio Forth prior to the station going on air as Head of News, becoming Programme Controller in 1978. His entire working life has been spent in journalism and broadcasting.

Non-Executive Director: Robert McPherson is Assistant Controller of Programmes for Scottish Television, based at the company's Edinburgh studios.

Non-Executive Director: Kenneth Baker is Chairman of the United Kingdom subsidiary of the Canadian broadcasting group, Selkirk Communications Ltd., and a Vice President of the main company.

Non-Executive Director: Joseph Currie is the Chief Executive Officer of the Scottish Midland Cooperative Society.

Non-Executive Director: Wendy Blakey, JP, is a member of the Industrial Tribunals for Scotland and has lectured extensively on management studies and public administration.

Non-Executive Director: John Romanes is the former managing Director of one of the leading newspaper groups in Fife.

Non-Executive Director: Alexander McEwen is the Personnel and Property Director of John Menzies PLC and was a professional musician.

Non-Executive Director: Lady Dunpark is a recently retired Edinburgh city councillor and is Convener of the Royal National Life Boat Institution.

Non-Executive Director: Donald Ford is an ex-professional footballer and now a financial consultant.